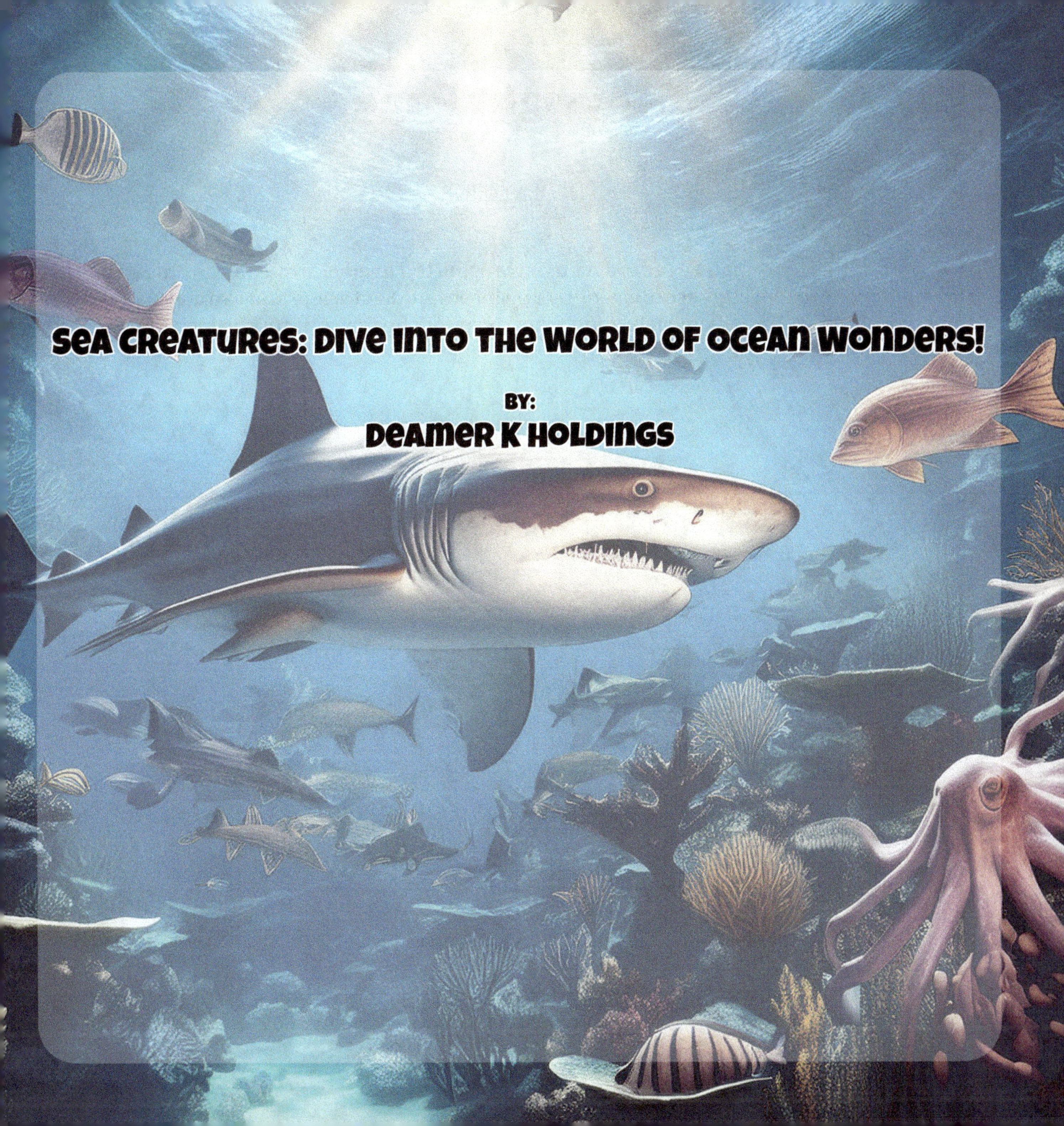

SEA CREATURES: DIVE INTO THE WORLD OF OCEAN WONDERS!
BY:
DEAMER K HOLDINGS

Copyright Page

© [2025] [Deamer K Holdings]
All Rights Reserved.

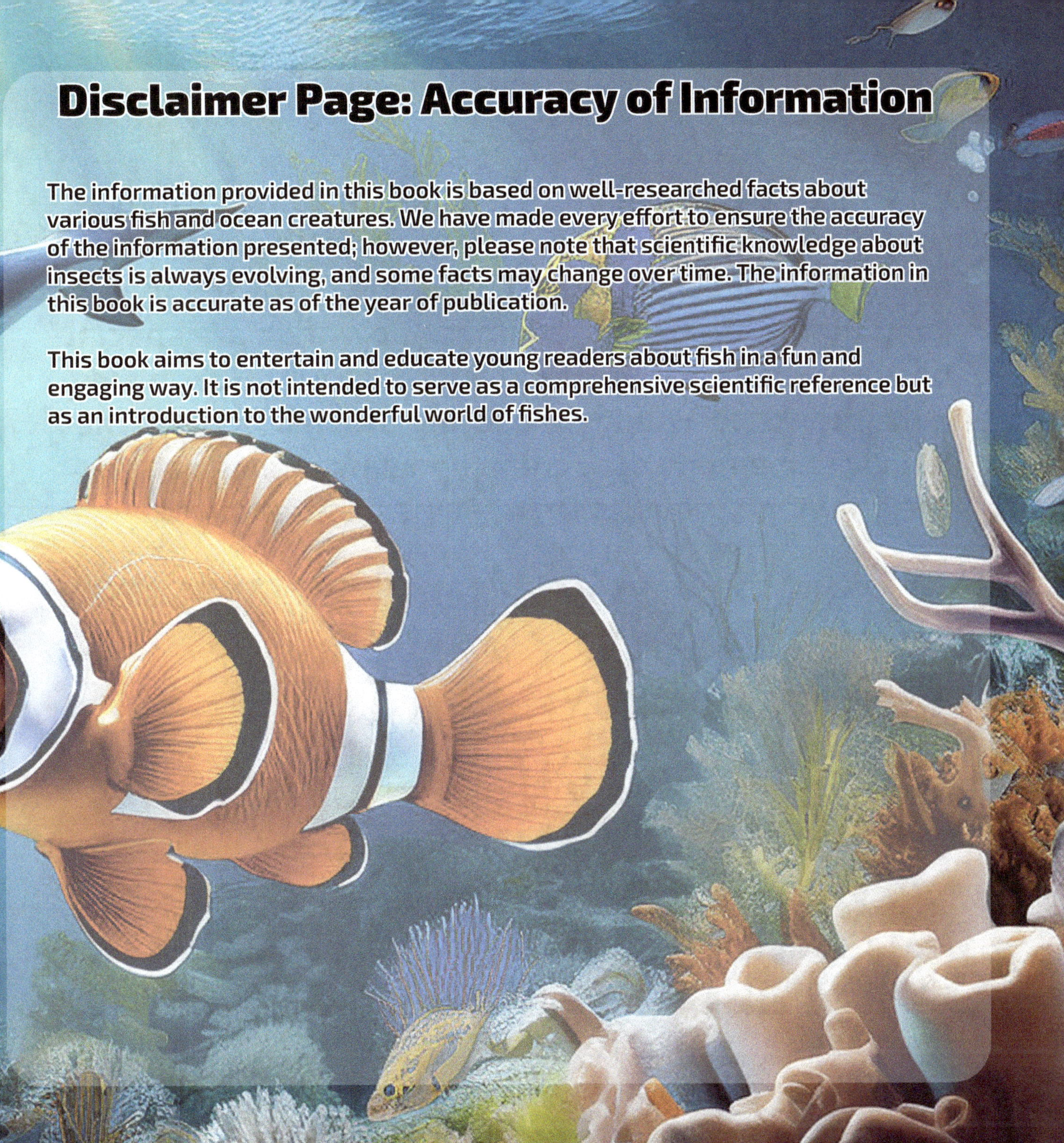

Disclaimer Page: Accuracy of Information

The information provided in this book is based on well-researched facts about various fish and ocean creatures. We have made every effort to ensure the accuracy of the information presented; however, please note that scientific knowledge about insects is always evolving, and some facts may change over time. The information in this book is accurate as of the year of publication.

This book aims to entertain and educate young readers about fish in a fun and engaging way. It is not intended to serve as a comprehensive scientific reference but as an introduction to the wonderful world of fishes.

Clownfish are small, orange fish with white stripes that live in the ocean. They make their homes in sea anemones, which have soft, stinging tentacles that keep them safe from predators. Clownfish are special because they can live in the anemone without getting hurt, thanks to a slippery coating on their bodies. They help the anemone stay clean and safe, and in return, the anemone protects them—a perfect teamwork!

CLOWNFISH – THE CORAL CUTIE

Clownfish – The Coral Cutie

Fun Facts:

- Clownfish have a special mucus layer that protects them from anemone stings.
- They communicate by making popping and clicking noises.
- All clownfish are born male, and some change to female as needed.

Goldfish are shiny, orange fish that often live in ponds or tanks as pets. They are known for their wiggly tails and big eyes that help them see their surroundings. Goldfish love to eat tiny plants or fish food and can grow to be much bigger if they have lots of space. They're fun to watch as they swim around, blowing bubbles and exploring their watery home!

GOLDFISH – THE GLITTERING FRIEND

Goldfish – The Glittering Friend

Fun Facts:

- Goldfish have a memory span of several months, not just 3 seconds.
- They can see more colors than humans, including ultraviolet light.
- Goldfish can grow up to a foot long in the wild!

Angelfish are beautiful, colorful fish with long, flowing fins that make them look like they're gliding through the water. They come in many patterns, like stripes and spots, and can be found in warm rivers or aquariums. Angelfish are curious and like to explore their surroundings, sometimes hiding in plants or coral. They are fun to watch because of their graceful swimming and bright colors!

ANGELFISH - THE OCEAN ROYALTY

Angelfish – The Ocean Royalty

Fun Facts:

- Angelfish can change colors as they grow older.
- They use their thin bodies to weave through coral reefs.
- These fish are found in both freshwater and saltwater environments.

Sharks are big, powerful fish that live in oceans all over the world. They have sharp teeth and strong bodies that help them swim fast and catch their food, like fish and squid. Some sharks, like the great white, are really big, while others, like the bamboo shark, are small and shy. Even though they might seem scary, most sharks are not dangerous to people and are important for keeping the ocean healthy!

SHARK - THE MIGHTY HUNTER

Shark – The Mighty Hunter

Fun Facts:

- Sharks have been around for over 400 million years.
- They can sense electrical fields produced by other animals.
- Most sharks have multiple rows of teeth that constantly replace themselves.

Seahorses are tiny, magical-looking fish that live in the ocean and look like they're standing up! They use their curly tails to hold onto plants so they don't float away. Unlike most animals, the dads carry the baby seahorses in a pouch on their belly until they're ready to swim on their own. Seahorses are great at hiding because their bumpy bodies blend in with seaweed and coral!

SEAHORSE – THE TINY HORSE OF THE SEA

Seahorse – The Tiny Horse of the Sea

Fun Facts:

- Male seahorses carry the babies in their pouch until they are born.
- They swim upright, unlike most other fish.
- Seahorses can change color to blend into their surroundings.

Parrotfish are colorful fish that look like they're smil-ing because of their beak-like mouths, which they use to scrape algae off rocks and coral. They play an important role in the ocean by helping to keep coral reefs clean and healthy. Parrotfish also do something amazing—they nibble on coral and turn it into sand, helping to create beautiful sandy beaches! These fish are like underwater artists, adding vibrant colors to the reef with their bright scales.

PARROTFISH - THE REEF ARTIST

Parrotfish – The Reef Artist

Fun Facts:

- They use their teeth to scrape algae off coral, helping keep reefs healthy.
- Parrotfish poop out sand, creating beaches.
- Some parrotfish sleep in a mucus cocoon to hide from predators.

Pufferfish are amazing fish that can puff up into a big, round ball when they feel scared or in danger! They do this by quickly filling their tummies with water or air, making it hard for predators to eat them. Some pufferfish even have spines on their bodies to make them extra tricky to catch. These fascinating fish may look cute, but they are also one of the most poisonous creatures in the ocean!

PUFFERFISH – THE INFLATABLE WONDER

Pufferfish – The Inflatable Wonder

Fun Facts:

- Pufferfish inflate by swallowing water or air.
- Their spines contain a toxin called tetrodotoxin, which is 1,200 times deadlier than cyanide.
- Despite their defense mechanisms, they are poor swimmers.

Lionfish are beautiful fish with long, spiky fins that look like a lion's mane, which is how they got their name! They have colorful red, white, and brown stripes that make them easy to spot. Although they look friendly, lionfish can be dangerous because their spines are sharp and can hurt you if you touch them. These fish are also very good at hiding in coral reefs and hunting small animals like shrimp and fish.

LIONFISH – THE SPIKY BEAUTY

Lionfish – The Spiky Beauty

Fun Facts:

- Lionfish are invasive in many waters, eating smaller fish and disrupting ecosystems.
- Their venomous spines deter predators, but they aren't harmful to humans unless touched.
- They can eat prey up to half their size.

Eels are long, slimy fish that wiggle like snakes through the water. They have smooth, slippery bodies that help them slither into cracks and crevices in rocks or coral. Some eels, like moray eels, have sharp teeth and are great hunters, while others are gentle and spend most of their time hiding. Eels can be found in oceans, and they help keep the underwater world balanced by eating small creatures.

EEL - THE SLIPPERY SWIMMER

Eel – The Slippery Swimmer

Fun Facts:

- Some eels can deliver electric shocks to stun prey or defend themselves.
- Moray eels have a second set of jaws to help grab food.
- Eels are nocturnal hunters.

Starfish, also called sea stars, are fascinating creatures with five (or more) arms that look like a star. They move slowly along the ocean floor using tiny tube feet on the underside of their arms. Starfish can regrow lost arms, which helps them survive if they get hurt. They eat by turning their stomachs inside out to digest their food, like clams and mussels, right in their shells!

STARFISH – THE OCEAN STAR

Starfish – The Ocean Star

Fun Facts:

- Starfish can regenerate lost arms, and some species can regrow their entire body.
- They move using tiny tube feet on their underside.
- Starfish don't have brains or blood; they pump seawater through their bodies.

Catfish are known for their long, whisker-like barbels around their mouths, which help them find food in the water. They live in both freshwater and saltwater, and some species can grow very large! Catfish are bottom-dwellers, meaning they spend most of their time at the bottom of lakes or rivers searching for food. They are great at using their sense of touch to find food in murky water where they can't see well.

CATFISH – THE WHISKERED WANDERER

Catfish – The Whiskered Wanderer

Fun Facts:

- Catfish use their whiskers to sense food in murky water.
- Some species can "walk" on land by wiggling their bodies.
- They make grunting or squeaking noises to communicate.

Swordfish are large, powerful fish known for their long, flat "sword" that extends from the front of their heads. This sword helps them catch prey and defend themselves. They are fast swimmers and can travel great distances in the ocean. Swordfish live in warm waters and are often seen jumping out of the water when they are excited or chasing food.

SWORDFISH – THE SPEEDY FENCER

Swordfish – The Speedy Fencer

Fun Facts:

- Swordfish use their bills to slash at prey, stunning or injuring them.
- They can swim up to 60 miles per hour.
- Swordfish don't have scales as adults.

Guppies are small, colorful fish that are often kept in aquariums. They come in many bright colors like orange, blue, and yellow, and have beautiful patterns on their bodies. Guppies are very friendly and like to swim in groups called schools. They are easy to take care of and are great for beginners who want to keep fish as pets.

GUPPY – THE TINY RAINBOW

Guppy – The Tiny Rainbow

Fun Facts:

- Guppies are livebearers, meaning they give birth to live babies instead of laying eggs.
- They're known for their adaptability and can live in a wide range of environments.
- Male guppies are more colorful than females to attract mates.

The clown triggerfish is a colorful fish with bold, bright patterns on its body. It has a white and black checkered pattern, with a yellow tail and a big, round mouth. These fish are found in warm, tropical waters and like to hide in coral reefs. They are known for being playful and can even change the color of their skin to blend in with their surroundings!

CLOWN TRIGGERFISH – THE POLKA-DOT PERFORMER

Clown Triggerfish – The Polka-Dot Performer

Fun Facts:

- They use strong jaws to crack open shells of clams and sea urchins.
- When threatened, they "lock" themselves into crevices using their spines.
- They are solitary and fiercely territorial.

Tuna are fast and powerful fish that swim in big groups called schools. They have sleek, streamlined bodies that help them swim very quickly through the water. Tuna can grow very large and are known for their strong muscles, which help them travel long distances across the ocean. They are often seen in warm waters and are a favorite of many sea predators!

TUNA – THE SWIFT SWIMMER

Tuna – The Swift Swimmer

Fun Facts:

- Tuna can swim at speeds of up to 43 miles per hour.
- They are warm-blooded, unlike most other fish.
- Some tuna species migrate thousands of miles each year.

Dolphins are playful and smart animals that live in the ocean. They are known for their friendly behavior and often jump out of the water or ride the waves near boats. Dolphins live in groups called pods, where they work together to find food and protect each other. They can communicate with each other using clicks, whistles, and body movements!

DOLPHIN – THE PLAYFUL SWIMMER

Dolphin – The Playful Swimmer

Fun Facts:

- Dolphins can recognize themselves in mirrors, which shows their intelligence!
- They are known to use tools, like sponges, to protect their noses while foraging for food on the ocean floor.
- Dolphins sleep with one eye open to stay alert for danger.

An octopus is a fascinating sea animal with eight long arms that can stretch and squirm. They are very clever and can solve puzzles or hide in tight spaces to avoid danger. Octopuses can change the color and texture of their skin to blend into their surroundings, helping them stay safe from predators. They also have a soft body, which allows them to squeeze through small openings!

OCTOPUS – THE MASTER OF DISGUISE

Octopus – The Master of Disguise

Fun Facts:

- Octopuses have three hearts and blue blood!
- They can squeeze through tiny openings because their bodies don't have bones.
- Some octopuses can solve puzzles and escape from aquariums, showing off their amazing intelligence.

A jellyfish is a soft, squishy sea creature with a clear, bell-shaped body that can glow in the dark! They have long, trailing tentacles that they use to catch food, but they don't have a brain, heart, or bones. Jellyfish float in the water and can move by pulsating their body to push themselves forward. Some jellyfish can sting, so it's important to be careful if you ever see one in the ocean!

JELLYFISH - THE OCEAN DRIFTER

Jellyfish – The Ocean Drifter

Fun Facts:

- Jellyfish have been around for more than 500 million years, making them one of the oldest creatures on Earth!
- Some species of jellyfish are bioluminescent, meaning they can glow in the dark.
- Despite their soft, squishy bodies, some jellyfish can sting with powerful venom.

Sea turtles are large, gentle reptiles that live in the ocean. They have hard, protective shells that help keep them safe from predators. Sea turtles spend most of their lives swimming in the sea, but they come ashore to lay their eggs on beaches. They can live for many years and travel long distances across the ocean!

SEA TURTLE - THE ANCIENT TRAVELER

Sea Turtle – The Ancient Traveler

Fun Facts:

- Sea turtles can live to be over 100 years old!
- They return to the same beaches where they were born to lay their eggs.
- Some sea turtles, like the leatherback, can dive to depths of over 4,000 feet!

Whales are huge mammals that live in the ocean. They are the largest animals on Earth, and some species, like the blue whale, can grow longer than a school bus! Whales breathe air through blowholes on top of their heads, and they can dive deep into the ocean to find food. Some whales even travel long distances each year to find warmer waters for breeding.

WHALE - THE GIANT OF THE OCEAN

Whale – The Giant of the Ocean

Fun Facts:

- The blue whale is the largest animal ever known to have lived, reaching lengths of over 100 feet.
- Whales communicate with songs that can travel for miles underwater.
- Despite their size, whales feed mostly on tiny creatures like krill, using their baleen plates to filter food.

Manta rays are large, gentle creatures that glide through the ocean like underwater birds. They have wide, triangular fins that look like wings, which help them "fly" through the water. Manta rays feed by swimming with their mouths open, filtering tiny plankton and fish from the water. Even though they are big, they are friendly and harmless to humans.

MANTA RAY - THE GRACEFUL GLIDER

Manta Ray – The Graceful Glider

Fun Facts:

- Manta rays have the largest brains of any fish, which may contribute to their intelligence.
- Their wingspan can reach up to 29 feet!
- Manta rays are filter feeders, meaning they swim with their mouths open, collecting plankton and small fish.

Anglerfish are deep-sea fish known for their unique way of hunting. They have a glowing lure on top of their heads that they use to attract prey in the dark ocean. When fish swim near the light, the anglerfish quickly opens its mouth to catch them. These fish have big mouths and sharp teeth, helping them eat their prey once they've caught it.

ANGLERFISH – THE DEEP-SEA LURE

Anglerfish – The Deep-Sea Lure

Fun Facts:

- Anglerfish live in the deep, dark parts of the ocean where sunlight doesn't reach.
- The glowing light is produced by bacteria that live in the lure.
- Some anglerfish species are so deep in the ocean that they rarely, if ever, come into contact with humans.

Lobsters are ocean creatures with hard, crunchy shells and long antennae. They use their powerful claws to catch food and protect themselves from predators. Lobsters are great at hiding in small crevices and caves on the ocean floor. They grow by shedding their shells and growing new, bigger ones.

LOBSTER – THE OCEAN SCAVENGER

Lobster – The Ocean Scavenger

Fun Facts:

- Lobsters can live up to 50 years and grow throughout their lives by molting, or shedding their exoskeleton.
- Their claws are strong enough to crack open shells and other tough food.
- Lobsters can regenerate lost limbs over time!

Squids are ocean animals that look like big, soft fish with eight arms and two long tentacles. They can squirt ink to escape from danger, which makes it hard for predators to see them. Squids are fast swimmers and can change color to blend in with their surroundings. They have small, sharp beaks to catch and eat their food.

SQUID – THE SWIFT SWIMMER

Squid – The Swift Swimmer

Fun Facts:

- Squids have three hearts and blue blood!
- Some squid species can change color and even create clouds of ink to escape predators.
- The giant squid can grow to be over 40 feet long, but it's rarely seen by humans.

Coloring
Pages

Draw Your Own Fish

What kind of fish would you create?

Draw and color your fish in the space. Don't forget to give it a name and tell us something fun about it!"

Draw Your Own Fish

What kind of fish would you create?

Draw and color your fish in the space. Don't forget to give it a
name and tell us something fun about it!"

Draw Your Own Fish

What kind of fish would you create?

Draw and color your fish in the space. Don't forget to give it a name and tell us something fun about it!"

Draw Your Own Fish

What kind of fish would you create?

Draw and color your fish in the space. Don't forget to give it a name and tell us something fun about it!"

Draw Your Own Fish
What kind of fish would you create?

Draw and color your fish in the space. Don't forget to give it a name and tell us something fun about it!"

Draw Your Own Fish

What kind of fish would you create?

Draw and color your fish in the space. Don't forget to give it a name and tell us something fun about it!"

Glossary

Learn more about the fish and terms in your book!

1. **Aquatic**
Relating to water; something that lives or grows in water.
2. **Bioluminescence**
The ability of some animals, like jellyfish and squids, to glow in the dark underwater.
3. **Camouflage**
A way animals blend in with their surroundings to hide from predators or sneak up on prey.
4. **Claws**
The sharp pincers found on animals like lobsters and crabs, used for catching food or defending themselves.
5. **Coral Reef**
A colorful underwater habitat made by tiny animals called coral that provide a home for many sea creatures.
6. **Ecosystem**
A community of plants, animals, and their environment, like the ocean, working together.
7. **Habitat**
The natural home where an animal or plant lives, such as the sandy ocean floor or a coral reef.
8. **Invertebrate**
An animal without a backbone, like a jellyfish, octopus, or starfish.
9. **Jet Propulsion**
A method of movement where animals like squids and octopuses shoot out water to push themselves forward.
10. **Marine**
Relating to the ocean or sea.
11. **Predator**
An animal that hunts and eats other animals.
12. **Prey**
An animal that is hunted and eaten by predators.
13. **School**
A group of fish swimming together.

Glossary

This glossary will provide a helpful resource for kids to learn new words and understand the fascinating world of sea creatures!

14. Tentacles
Long, flexible limbs used by animals like octopuses and jellyfish to catch food or sense their environment.

15. Plankton
Tiny plants and animals that float in the water and are eaten by many sea creatures, like whales and fish.

16. Beak
A hard, sharp mouthpart found in creatures like parrotfish and squids, used for eating food.

17. Sand
Tiny grains of rock and shell found on the ocean floor or beaches.

18. Suction Cups
Small, sticky circles found on the tentacles of octopuses, used to grab and hold objects.

19. Tide Pool
A small pool of water left on the shore when the tide goes out, often full of interesting sea creatures.

20. Whale Song
The sounds made by whales to communicate with each other underwater.

21. Filter Feeder
An animal that eats by straining tiny food particles from water, like some whales and starfish.

22. Gills
The part of a fish that helps it breathe underwater by taking in oxygen from the water.

23. Fins
The body parts of fish that help them swim and balance in the water.

24. Shell
The hard, protective covering of animals like lobsters, crabs, and clams.

25. Buoyancy
The ability of something to float in water.

Parent's Notes

Dear Parents and Caregivers,

Thank you for choosing our "Sea Creatures" book! This book is designed to introduce young children to the magical world beneath the waves. It offers fascinating facts, vibrant illustrations, and engaging activities that will inspire curiosity about the ocean and its incredible inhabitants.

We encourage you to use this book as a tool for fostering a love of marine life and sparking meaningful conversations about the wonders of the sea. Learning about ocean creatures can teach children about nature, science, and the importance of protecting our planet's ecosystems.

Suggestions for Use:

 Ask your child which sea creature they think is the most interesting or unique and why.
 Use the fun facts to start discussions about how sea creatures survive and thrive in their underwater homes.
 Encourage your child to draw their favorite sea creature or imagine an underwater scene full of colorful marine life.
We hope that through this book, your child will develop a love for the ocean and a deeper appreciation for the incredible creatures that call it home!

Sincerely,
The Playful Planet Team

Thank You Page

A Special Thank You

Thank you for bringing "Sea Creatures" into your home! We are so excited that your child is learning about the wonderful world of bugs. We hope this book has sparked curiosity, excitement, and an appreciation for the small but mighty creatures that share our world.

A big thank you goes to the talented illustrators, designers, and everyone who helped bring this book to life. Without their hard work, this book would not be possible.

Thank you for supporting our work! We look forward to bringing you more fun, educational books in the future.

With gratitude,
Playful Planet Kids Show

Leave a Review Page

We'd Love to Hear Your Thoughts!

If you and your little one enjoyed "Sea Creatures" we would greatly appreciate it if you could leave a review! Your feedback helps us improve and helps other families discover our books.

To leave a review:

Visit https://www.amazon.com/stores/author/B0CXMJXRVK].
Click on the "Write a Review" button.
Share your thoughts on what you liked most about the book and how your child enjoyed it.
Thank you for your support!
We truly appreciate your feedback, and it helps us create even more fun and educational books for kids!

Social Media Page

Stay Connected!

We'd love to see how your child is enjoying the bug world and learning about all kinds of Sea Creatures! Share your experiences and connect with us on social media:

Follow us:

Instagram: @[playfulplanetkidsshow]
Facebook: @[playfulplanetkidsshow]
Twitter: @[playfulplanetkidsshow]
Tik Tok: @[playfulplanetkidsshow]
Don't forget to tag us when your little one is out bug hunting or enjoying their new book! We may feature your photos on our social media pages!

#PlayfulplanetKidsshow

PLAYFUL PLANET
KIDS SHOW